Robinson Cano

By Jon M. Fishman

Lerner Publications ◆ Minneapolis

Copyright © 2016 by Lerner Publishing Group, Inc.

All rights reserved. International copyright secured. No part of this book may be reproduced, stored in a retrieval system, or transmitted in any form or by any means—electronic, mechanical, photocopying, recording, or otherwise—without the prior written permission of Lerner Publishing Group, Inc., except for the inclusion of brief quotations in an acknowledged review.

Lerner Publications Company
A division of Lerner Publishing Group, Inc.
241 First Avenue North
Minneapolis, MN 55401 USA

For reading levels and more information, look up this title at www.lernerbooks.com.

Library of Congress Cataloging-in-Publication Data

Names: Fishman, Jon M.
Title: Robinson Cano / by Jon M. Fishman.
Description: Minneapolis : Lerner Publications, [2016] | Series: Amazing athletes | Includes bibliographical references, webography and index.
Identifiers: LCCN 2015035217 | ISBN 9781467793858 (lb : alk. paper) | ISBN 9781467796194 (pb : alk. paper) | ISBN 9781467796200 (eb pdf)
Subjects: LCSH: Cano, Robinson, 1982– —Juvenile literature. | Baseball players—Dominican Republic—Biography—Juvenile literature.
Classification: LCC GV865.C312 F57 2016 | DDC 796.357092—dc23
LC record available at http://lccn.loc.gov/2015035217

Manufactured in the United States of America
1 – BP – 12/31/15

TABLE OF CONTENTS

Mariners Masher	4
The Boy with No Name	9
Getting Paid	14
The Big Leagues	19
Home Run Champ	24
Selected Career Highlights	29
Glossary	30
Further Reading & Websites	31
Index	32

Robinson Cano runs the bases after he hits a home run against the Boston Red Sox.

MARINERS MASHER

Seattle Mariners **second baseman** Robinson Cano stepped to the plate in the first inning. He and his teammates were playing against the Boston Red Sox on August 16, 2015. With a runner on third base, the pitcher fired the ball. Robinson let loose with a lightning-quick swing. *Smack!* The ball soared through the air and over the outfield wall for a **home run**. Seattle took the lead, 2–0.

Robinson next came to bat in the third inning with his team ahead, 3–0. The Mariners had runners on second base and third base.

Robinson at bat for the Seattle Mariners

> The Mariners are one of eight teams that have never won the World Series. The others are the Texas Rangers, the Tampa Bay Rays, the Houston Astros, the Washington Nationals, the Milwaukee Brewers, the Colorado Rockies, and the San Diego Padres.

Robinson stroked a single to left field for another **run batted in (RBI)**. Then Franklin Gutierrez crushed a home run. Seattle had a huge lead, 7–0.

Robinson hit a **single** in the fifth inning. Then he knocked a **double** in the seventh inning. But Boston was catching up. They tied the game in the bottom of the ninth inning, 8–8. The game would go into extra innings to break the tie.

With a single, a double, and a home run in the game, Robinson needed a **triple** to complete the **cycle**. The cycle is a rare feat in baseball. In the 11th inning, Robinson came to bat with a chance to make history. He swung and made contact with the ball. It streaked up the middle for a single. It wasn't the triple fans had been hoping for, but it was the fifth hit of the game for Robinson. He had never had five hits in a game in his 14-year career.

Smacking five hits in a game is rare, even for great players like Robinson.

The Mariners finally scored two runs in the 12th inning and won the game. It was another big day at the ballpark for Robinson. The superstar second baseman has won tons of awards and honors in **Major League Baseball (MLB)**. With a **contract** that goes until 2023, Robinson will be helping Seattle win games for a long time to come.

Robinson celebrates his two-run home run.

San Pedro de Macoris is in the southeastern part of the Dominican Republic.

THE BOY WITH NO NAME

On October 22, 1982, a baby boy was born in San Pedro de Macoris, Dominican Republic. His parents, Jose Cano and Claribel Mercedes, couldn't agree on a name. The couple argued about it for weeks, and still the baby had no name.

> Jackie Robinson played for the Dodgers from 1947 to 1956. He was the first African American to play in the major leagues.

Jose was a professional baseball player. He wanted to name his son in honor of Brooklyn Dodgers legend Jackie Robinson. Claribel wasn't so sure she wanted her son named after a baseball player. But finally, she agreed. They named the child Robinson.

> Jackie Robinson was voted into the Baseball Hall of Fame in 1962.

Jose urged Robinson to play baseball. The boy liked the sport. Jose was a pitcher, but Robinson preferred to swing the bat. He had quick hands and a smooth style. Robinson and Jose practiced together when they could. But Jose was away from home a lot. He played baseball in Mexico. In 1989, he moved to the United States and played six games with the Houston Astros.

Jose (*right*) continued to encourage Robinson throughout his career.

Warm temperatures in the Dominican Republic allow kids to play baseball there all year.

GETTING PAID

With plenty of opportunity to play baseball in the Dominican Republic, Robinson quickly grew into a promising young player. He had thick legs and didn't run fast. But he had a strong throwing arm and always knew where he was supposed to be on the field.

As a batter, Robinson's skills really shined. He was incredibly quick and smacked the ball all around the field. He also had enough power in his bat to knock balls over the outfield fence for home runs.

Professional **scouts** liked what they saw in Robinson. Gordon Blakeley of the New York Yankees was especially interested. In 2001, after Robinson graduated from high school, the team offered Robinson a contract worth $150,000.

Scout Gordon Blakeley thought Robinson had the skills to play for the Yankees someday.

> Almost 40 MLB players have come from San Pedro de Macoris, including Sammy Sosa and Alfonso Soriano.

But Jose wasn't happy with the offer. "He said his son was worth a lot more," Blakeley said. The scout convinced the Canos to take the deal. He told them that Robinson would have the chance to earn a lot more money in the years to come.

Robinson's first professional games were in the **minor leagues**.

> Like Robinson, former Yankees star Alfonso Soriano (*right*) came from San Pedro de Macoris.

In 2001, he played for the Gulf Coast League Yankees and the Staten Island Yankees. In 59 total games, Robinson's **batting average** was just .231. He hit only three home runs all year.

It was clear that Robinson had a lot to learn before he would be ready to play in the major leagues. Bill Masse was a **manager** for a minor-league team at the time.

Robinson had work to do in the minor leagues before he would be ready to play for the Yankees.

Robinson poses in his New York Yankees uniform.

He noticed that the young player didn't put in much work before games. "[Robinson] wanted to show up at 6:55 and play at 7:00," Masse said. It wasn't that Robinson was unwilling to work to get better. It was just that in the past he had never needed to work hard to be one of the best players on his team.

Robinson's batting improved when he began to work harder.

THE BIG LEAGUES

In 2002, Robinson began the year back with Staten Island. But before long, he moved up a level to play with the Greensboro Bats, a more advanced minor-league team. Robinson had learned that working hard on his baseball skills and fitness would make him a better player. For the season, his batting average improved to .276. He also swatted 15 home runs.

Over the next two years, Robinson continued to sharpen his baseball abilities. Then, early in the 2005 season, he was called up to play with the New York Yankees. On May 4, he came to bat with a runner on first base. Robinson swung and sent a bouncing ball into the outfield for his first major-league hit.

> Robinson turned himself into a very hard worker. When he isn't playing baseball, he often gets up at dawn to run, lift weights, and practice hitting and fielding.

Robinson finished his first year with the Yankees with a .297 batting average and 14 home runs. In 2006, he was even better. He hit an incredible .342 and smashed 15 home runs. Fans voted for Robinson to play in his first **All-Star Game**.

The Yankees are the most successful team

Robinson was voted into the All-Star Game during his second major-league season.

in MLB history. They have won the World Series 27 times, more than any other team. But they hadn't been to the World Series since losing to the Florida Marlins in 2003. In 2009, Robinson did his best to help his team win another championship. He hit .320 and blasted 25 home runs. The Yankees won 103 games and lost only 59.

Robinson helped the Yankees get to the World Series in 2009.

Then they charged through the **playoffs** to reach the World Series. They faced off against the Philadelphia Phillies.

The Yankees won three of the first five games against the Phillies. In Game 6, New York had a four-run lead in the ninth inning. They sent superstar Mariano Rivera to the

pitching mound to try to end the game. With two outs, Phillies outfielder Shane Victorino hit a bouncing ball. Robinson scooped it up and flipped the ball to first base for the out.

He raised both arms and leaped into the air. The Yankees were world champions!

Robinson and his teammates celebrate their World Series win.

Robinson swings for a home run in the final round of the 2011 Home Run Derby.

HOME RUN CHAMP

In 2011, fans voted Robinson to the All-Star Game for the third time. He also agreed to swing in the Home Run Derby. The derby is held just before the All-Star Game each year. Players choose someone to pitch to them and then compete to see who can launch the most home runs. Robinson chose his dad as his pitcher.

Robinson and Jose worked well together. The **slugger** blasted home run after home run into the night sky. In the final round, he smacked 11 home runs. It was enough to win the derby! Robinson gave all the credit to his dad. "I don't want to say that I won the trophy," Robinson said. "I want to say that my dad has won the trophy."

Robinson lifts his Home Run Derby trophy high in the air.

Robinson had become known as a great player on the field. But he received praise for his work off the field as well. In 2005, the Yankees had visited a hospital in Hackensack, New Jersey. Robinson made friends with a young patient at the hospital who had cancer.

Robinson (*right*) and teammate Melky Cabrera (*left*) pose with hospital patient Jack Szigety (*center*).

Robinson continued to visit patients in the hospital. He also helped the hospital raise money. In 2011, they named part of the hospital in Robinson's honor. "Everyone knows one of the things Robinson does best is hit home runs . . . but best of all is how he hits them off the field too," said Robert C. Garrett, president of the hospital. Robinson also started the RC22 Foundation. The group works to provide children in the Dominican Republic with education, and it also works with hospitals in the United States.

> Author Ray Negron was inspired by the time Robinson spent at the hospital in New Jersey. In 2006, Negron wrote a children's book about it called *The Boy of Steel: A Baseball Dream Come True.*

After the 2013 season, Robinson's contract with the Yankees ended. He was free to join any team. The Mariners offered him a deal worth $240 million! At the time, it was tied for the fourth-largest contract in baseball history. Jose Cano may not have been happy with his son's first contract back in 2001. But with natural talent and hard work, Robinson turned himself into a superstar and one of the top-paid athletes in the world.

Robinson joined the Seattle Mariners after his years with the Yankees.

Selected Career Highlights

2015 Had five hits in a single game for the first time

2014 Named to the All-Star Game for the sixth time
Finished fifth in voting for American League Most Valuable Player

2013 Named to the All-Star Game for the fifth time
Finished fifth in voting for American League Most Valuable Player
Agreed to a $240 million contract with the Mariners

2012 Named to the All-Star Game for the fourth time
Won the Gold Glove Award as best fielding second baseman in the American League
Finished fourth in voting for American League Most Valuable Player

2011 Named to the All-Star Game for the third time
Finished sixth in voting for American League Most Valuable Player
Was honored by a New Jersey hospital for his work with children

2010 Named to the All-Star Game for the second time
Won the Gold Glove Award as best fielding second baseman in the American League
Finished third in voting for American League Most Valuable Player

2009 Helped the Yankees win the World Series

2006 Named to the All-Star Game for the first time

2005 Played his first MLB game

2001 Signed his first professional contract

Glossary

All-Star Game: a game featuring top MLB players, played in the middle of each season

batting average: a number that describes how often a baseball player gets a hit

contract: an agreement signed by a player and a team that states the amount of money the player is paid and the number of years he plays

cycle: hitting a single, a double, a triple, and a home run in the same game

double: a hit that allows a player to reach second base

home run: a hit that allows a batter to run all the way around the bases to score a run

Major League Baseball (MLB): the top level of professional baseball in the United States and Canada

manager: the head coach of a baseball team

minor leagues: a series of teams in which players gain experience and improve their skills before going to the major leagues

pitching mound: the raised area in the middle of a baseball diamond where the pitcher stands

playoffs: a series of games held to decide a champion

run batted in (RBI): a statistic that gives credit to a player for making a play that allows a runner to score

scouts: people who judge the skills of players

second baseman: a player who stands between first base and second base

single: a hit that allows a batter to reach first base

slugger: a batter who hits lots of home runs

triple: a hit that allows a batter to reach third base

Further Reading & Websites

Berne, Emma Carlson. *What's Your Story, Jackie Robinson?* Minneapolis: Lerner Publications, 2016.

Braun, Eric. *Super Baseball Infographics*. Minneapolis: Lerner Publications, 2015.

Fishman, Jon M. *Mariano Rivera*. Minneapolis: Lerner Publications, 2014.

Kennedy, Mike, and Mark Stewart. *Long Ball: The Legend and Lore of the Home Run*. Minneapolis: Millbrook Press, 2006.

The Official Site of Major League Baseball
http://www.mlb.com/home
Major League Baseball's official website provides fans with the latest scores and game schedules, as well as information on players, teams, and baseball history.

The Official Site of the Seattle Mariners
http://www.mariners.com
The Seattle Mariners' official site includes the team schedule and game results. Visitors can also find late-breaking news, biographies of Robinson Cano and other players and coaches, and much more.

Sports Illustrated Kids
http://www.sikids.com
The *Sports Illustrated Kids* website covers all sports, including baseball.

Expand learning beyond the printed book. Download free, complementary educational resources for this book from our website, www.lerneresource.com.

Index

Blakeley, Gordon, 15–16
Boston Red Sox, 4

Cano, Jose, 9–13, 16, 25, 28

Dominican Republic, 9, 13, 14, 27

Greensboro Bats, 19
Gulf Coast League Yankees, 17
Gutierrez, Franklin, 6

Masse, Bill, 17–18
Mercedes, Claribel, 9–10, 12

Newark, New Jersey, 12–13
New York Yankees, 15, 20–23, 26, 28

Philadelphia Phillies, 22–23

RC22 Foundation, 27
Rivera, Mariano, 22
Robinson, Jackie, 10

San Pedro de Macoris, 9, 16
Seattle Mariners, 4–5, 8, 28
Staten Island Yankees, 17

Victorino, Shane, 23

World Series, 6, 21–23

Photo Acknowledgments

The images in this book are used with the permission of: © Jim Rogash/Getty Images, p. 4; © Winslow Townson/USA TODAY Sports, pp. 5, 7; AP Photo/Michael Dwyer, p. 8; © Hemis/Alamy, p. 9; © Hulton Archive/Getty Images, p. 10; AP Photo/David J. Phillip, p. 11; © John Van Decker/Alamy, p. 12; © Terrence Antonio James/Chicago Tribune/TNS/Alamy, p. 14; © Andrew Savulich/NY Daily News Archive/Getty Images, p. 15; © Tom Pidgeon/Getty Images, p. 16; © Linda Cataffo/NY Daily News Archive/Getty Images, p. 17; © Ezra Shaw/Getty Images, p. 18; AP Photo/Ed Betz, p. 19; © John Reid III/MLB Photos/Getty Images, p. 21; © Nick Laham/Getty Images, p. 22; © Chris McGrath/Getty Images, p. 23; © Norm Hall/Getty Images, p. 24; © Jeff Gross/Getty Images, p. 25; © Corey Sipkin/NY Daily News Archive/Getty Images, p. 26; © Rich Schultz/Getty Images, p. 28; © Denis Poroy/Getty Images, p. 29.

Front cover: © Otto Greule Jr/Getty Images.

Main body text set in Caecilia LT Std 55 Roman 16/28.
Typeface provided by Adobe Systems.